HARCOURT ART EVERYWHERE

AUTHORS

Jacqueline Chanda

Kristen Pederson Marstaller

CONSULTANTS

Katherina Danko-McGhee

María Teresa García-Pedroche

Harcourt

SCHOOL PUBLISHERS

Orlando   Austin   New York   San Diego   Toronto   London

Visit *The Learning Site!*
www.harcourtschool.com

Printed in the United States of America

ISBN 0-15-336446-7

2 3 4 5 6 7 8 9 10   048   13 12 11 10 09 08 07 06 05

Dear Young Artist,

The art in this book comes from all over the world. Some of it is very old. Some was made a short time ago. All of the art tells something about the people who made it.

Art is all around you. Have fun looking at, thinking about, and making art.

Sincerely,

The Authors

CONTENTS

Unit 1 — The World Around Me 22
Line and Shape

AT A GLANCE

Art Production

Elements and Principles

Media

Cross-Curricular Connections

Artists make sketches.

They use their sketches to make art.

But when
his bell jingles,
birds call a
loud warning:

WHISTLE
WHISTLE
CHECK
CHECK
CHECK

Northern Oriole

Lilac bush

JINGLE
JINGLE

▲ from *Feathers for Lunch*   LITERATURE LINK
by Lois Ehlert

Keep an art sketchbook. Put pictures, colors, and words in it.

Draw what you see.
Make sketches.

Visiting a Museum

▲ Kimball Art Museum, Fort Worth, Texas

Walk slowly.

▲ Baltimore Museum of Art, Baltimore, Maryland

Look and think.
Ask questions.

▲ Corcoran Gallery of Art, Washington, D.C.

Talk quietly.

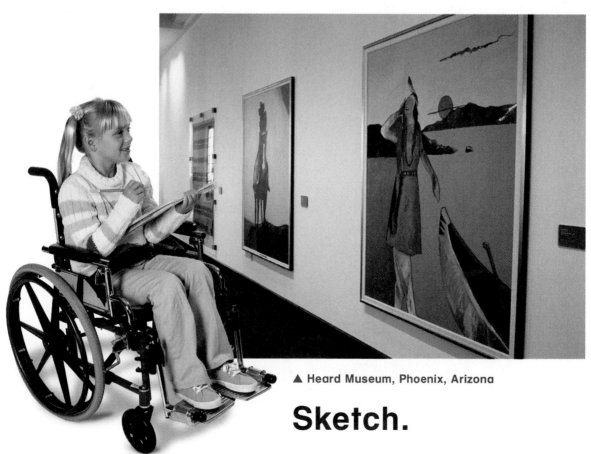

▲ Heard Museum, Phoenix, Arizona

Sketch.

A **title** tells what a lesson is about.

Lesson
3

Vocabulary

shapes

Lines Make Shapes

What do you see in this artwork?

A **caption** tells the name of the artist and artwork.

Paul Klee, *Castle and Sun*

Artists join lines to make **shapes**. What shapes do the lines make?

A **highlighted word** helps you learn art vocabulary.

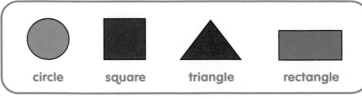

circle   square   triangle   rectangle

32

Look for other important parts of your book.
- Title Page
- Contents
- Glossary

Artist's Workshop

Neighborhood Collage

PLAN

Think about shapes you can use to show your neighborhood.

CREATE

The **steps** are in order. They tell how to make an artwork.

1. Cut out paper shapes.

2. Group the shapes. Then glue them.

REFLECT

What shapes did you use? Why?

What shapes do you see around you?

33

Elements and Principles

Elements of Art

Art is made up of parts called **elements**. Here are elements you will explore.

line ▲

value ▲

shape ▼

color ▲

See also Elements and
Principles, pages 172–183.

texture ▼

space ▲

Grade A Fancy
**GREEN
SWEET PEAS**

NET WT. 8.5 OZ (241 g)

form ▲

19

Principles of Design

Artists use art elements according to **principles**. Here are principles you will learn about.

pattern ▼

variety ▲

emphasis ▲

See also Elements and Principles, pages 172–183.

unity ▼

balance ▲

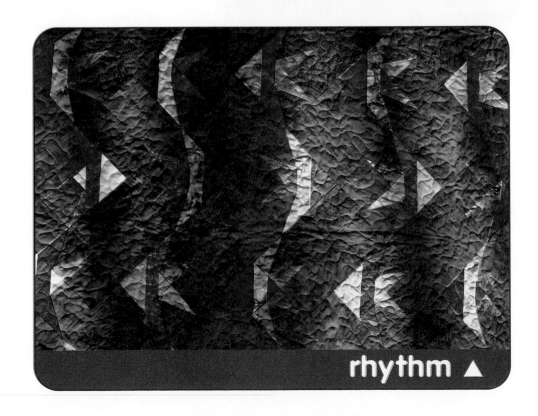

rhythm ▲

▲ Gabriele Münter, *Staffelsee in Autumn*

LOCATE IT

This painting is in the National Museum of Women in the Arts in Washington, D.C.

See Maps of Museums and Art Sites, pages 144–147.

Washington, D.C.

The World Around Me

From My Window

From my window

I can see

The whole world

Waiting for me.

A fresh, bright day

Beginning, new.

Oh, come and look!

I'll share with you.

Joan Walsh Anglund

Unit Vocabulary

lines   still life

zigzag   portrait

shapes   self-portrait

free-form
  shapes

ABOUT THE ARTIST

See Gallery of Artists,
pages 184–191.

GO ONLINE

Multimedia Art Glossary
Visit *The Learning Site*
www.harcourtschool.com

23

Note Details

What does this painting show?
Look closer. What do you see?

Carmen Lomas Garza, *Empanadas/Tío Beto y Tía Paz,*
from *In My Family* LITERATURE LINK

The small parts of this painting
are **details**.

Make a web. Add details.

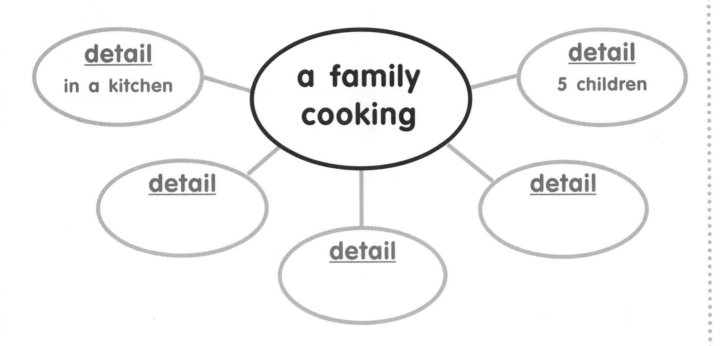

Look at the painting on pages 22–23.
Make a web. Draw or write details.

Lines in My World

What do you see in this art?

A Alexander Calder,
Bird ornament

B Henri Matisse,
Still Life with Pomegranates

Lines are everywhere. Artists use **lines**. Find lines like these.

thin   thick   slanted   curved   zigzag

"From My Window" Drawing

PLAN ··

Think of a favorite outdoor place.

CREATE ···

1. Draw a window the size of your paper.

2. Use lines to draw your favorite place.

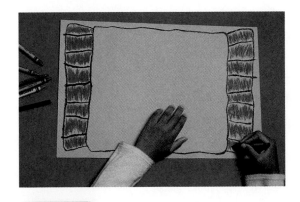

REFLECT ··

What kinds of lines did you use? Why?

What kinds of lines do you see in your classroom?

Lines Show Motion

What is happening in each picture? What is moving?

A Vincent van Gogh,
The Starry Night

Use a finger to show how lines curve
or **zigzag** in the paintings.

Artists can use lines to make things look as if they are moving.

▲ **B** Georgia O'Keeffe,
From the Plains I

Artist's Workshop

Weather Painting

1. **Paint a picture of weather.**

2. **Use lines to show things moving.**

Van Gogh's World

A *The Bedroom at Arles*

Vincent van Gogh was a painter. He painted many pictures of himself and the places he lived.

Van Gogh sometimes painted himself in his paintings. Look for him on his bedroom wall.

 B Self-Portrait

 C *Road with Cypress and Star*

Think About Art

Why did Vincent van Gogh paint pictures of the places he lived?

 GO ONLINE

Multimedia Biographies
Visit *The Learning Site*
www.harcourtschool.com

Lines Make Shapes

What do you see in this artwork?

Paul Klee, *Castle and Sun*

Artists join lines to make **shapes**.
What shapes do the lines make?

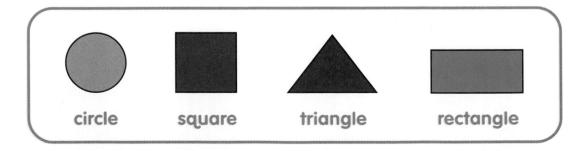

circle   square   triangle   rectangle

Neighborhood Collage

PLAN

Think about shapes you can use to show your neighborhood.

CREATE

1. Cut out paper shapes.

2. Group the shapes. Then glue them.

REFLECT

What shapes did you use? Why?

What shapes do you see around you?

All Kinds of Shapes

What do these artworks show?
How are they alike?

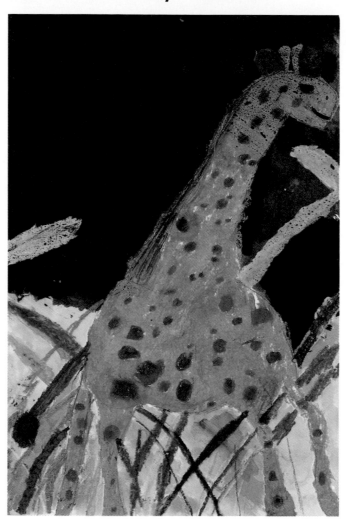

Hannah, grade 2,
Student art

Animals and many plants have
free-form shapes.

free-form shapes

This artwork is a **still life**. It shows a group of things that are not moving.

 Paul Cézanne,
Pot of Flowers and Pears

Artist's Workshop

Still-Life Drawing

1. **Put things with free-form shapes in a group.**

2. **Draw a still life.**

Art
All Around Us

Look around you. You can find lines and shapes everywhere.

Tell about the lines and shapes you see.

36

DID YOU KNOW?

You can learn about the world in many ways. What things in these pictures could you smell, touch, or hear?

Reunion Tower, Dallas, Texas

Think About Art

Which lines and shapes did people make?
Which ones were not made by people?

Shapes in Portraits

How are these paintings alike?

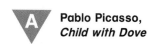 Pablo Picasso,
Child with Dove

 William H. Johnson,
Little Girl in Orange

A **portrait** is a picture of one or more people. A **self-portrait** is an artist's picture of himself or herself.

Framed Self-Portrait

PLAN

Think about something special you like to do.

CREATE

1. Draw yourself. Show something you like to do.

2. Make a frame for your art. Add shapes you like.

REFLECT

What shapes did you use? Why?

Unit 1 Review and Reflect

Vocabulary and Concepts

Tell which picture goes best with each word.

1. zigzag

2. lines

3. still life

4. free-form shapes

5. portrait

6. self-portrait

a.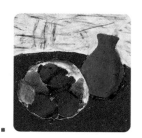

b.

c.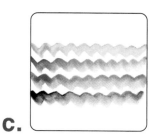

d.

e.

f.

7. Tell what kinds of lines you see.

a.

b.

c.

8. Name the shapes you see.

a.

b.

c.

Note Details

Look back at the painting on page 30. Tell details. Use the web to help you.

Van Gogh's bedroom

detail

detail

detail

Write About Art

Tell details about *The Starry Night*.

Lines around the moon make a circle.

Vincent van Gogh, *The Starry Night*

▲ Maurice Prendergast, *Summer, New England*

LOCATE IT

This painting is in the Smithsonian American Art Museum in Washington, D.C.

See Maps of Museums and Art Sites, pages 144–147.

Washington, D.C.

We Go Together

The More We Get Together

The more we get
together,
Together, together,
The more we get
together,
The happier we'll be.

Song

Unit Vocabulary

colors	value
color wheel	tints
warm colors	shade
cool colors	stained glass

ABOUT THE ARTIST

See Gallery of Artists, pages 184–191.

Multimedia Art Glossary
Visit *The Learning Site*
www.harcourtschool.com

Compare and Contrast

What animals are in this picture?
Tell which animals are the same.

Nancy Hom, illustration from *Nine-in-One, Grr! Grr!* LITERATURE LINK

Look at the birds.
How are they different?

Make a chart. Tell what is the same. Say what is different.

Same	Different
all birds in tree	tails of birds

On Your Own

Look at the painting on pages 42–43. Make a chart. Write what is the same and what is different.

The Color Wheel

What does this painting show?
Tell about the **colors** you see.

Marc Chagall,
I and the Village

Artists mix colors to make new colors.

A **color wheel** shows how you can mix colors.

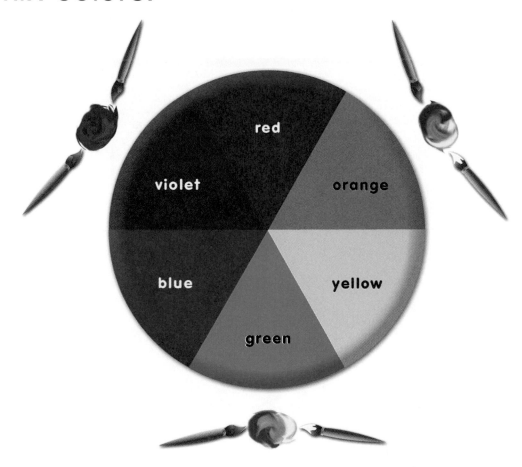

Painted Fan

1. Fold your paper. Paint three parts with red, yellow, and blue.

2. Mix colors to paint the other parts.

Warm and Cool Colors

Which painting looks warmer?

A Ernest Martin Hennings,
Afternoon Ride

Red, orange, and yellow are **warm colors**. They make a picture feel warm.

warm colors   cool colors

Rockwell Kent, *Snow Fields*
(Winter in the Berkshires) B ▶

Blue, green, and violet are **cool colors**.
They can make an artwork feel cool.

Artist's Workshop

Playground Art

1. Think of a playground
   in winter or summer.

2. Show how the place
   feels. Use warm colors
   or cool colors.

Diego Rivera's People

A *Children at Lunch*

Diego Rivera grew up in Mexico. He painted pictures of the people. He made wall paintings called **murals**.

B *Autorretrato (Self-Portrait)*

C **Still Life and Blossoming Almond Trees**

Think About Art

What can you learn about people in Diego Rivera's paintings?

Multimedia Biographies
Visit *The Learning Site*
www.harcourtschool.com

Making Colors Lighter

Where do you see light colors in this painting?

Pierre-Auguste Renoir,
Two Girls in Field

A color's lightness or darkness is its **value**. Artists make **tints**, or lighter colors, by adding white to colors.

Morning Painting

PLAN

Think about a sunny morning to paint.

CREATE

1. Use tints to paint your picture.

2. Add details using tints.

REFLECT

How did using tints help you show morning?

Where in your classroom can you see tints?

53

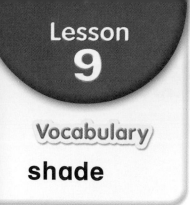

Making Colors Darker

Tell about the colors in the paintings.

A Anna Belle Lee Washington,
Mount Rainier Reflecting

B Adélaïde Labille-Guiard, *Portrait of Louise-
Elisabeth de France (1727–59), Duchess of
Parma and her son Ferdinand (1751–1802)*

Artists can make a **shade**, or darker
color, by adding black to a color.

Evening Painting

PLAN

Think of being home in the evening. How does the light make shadows?

CREATE

1. **Make shades to help you show nighttime.**

2. **Paint you and your family in the evening.**

REFLECT

What did you paint with shades? Why?

Look for light and dark colors at home and at school.

Eric Carle, Picture Writer

A Eric Carle, illustration from
Today Is Monday LITERATURE LINK

Eric Carle is a picture book
illustrator and writer. His job
is to make children's books.

First he paints tissue paper different colors. Then he cuts and glues the paper to make collages.

B Eric Carle

C Eric Carle, illustration from *Today Is Monday*

Think About Art

How can pictures help tell a story?

Stained Glass

How are these artworks alike?

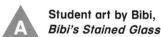
Student art by Bibi,
Bibi's Stained Glass

Unknown artist, Stained glass
at the Dowlat Abad Gardens

When light shines through
stained glass, you can see
colors and shapes.

58

Tissue Paper "Stained Glass"

PLAN

Think of colors and shapes you like.

CREATE

1. **Fold black paper. Cut out shapes.**

2. **Glue tissue paper behind each shape. Hold up to light.**

REFLECT

What happened when you held your artwork up to a light?

Vocabulary and Concepts

Tell which picture goes best with the word or words.

a.

b.

1. tint

2. stained glass

c.

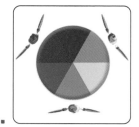
d.

3. shade

4. color wheel

· ·

5. Use the words <u>value</u>, <u>cool colors</u>, and <u>warm colors</u> to tell about the picture.

Compare and Contrast

Look at the paintings on pages 48 and 49. Tell how they are the same and different. Make a chart.

Same	Different

Write About Art

Write sentences that tell what is the same and different in the painting.

The trees are all
tall and green.

Anna Belle Lee Washington,
Mount Rainier Reflecting

▲ Unknown artist, *Mor Chowk* peacock mosaic,
City Palace, Udaipur, India

LOCATE IT

This mosaic is in the City Palace and Museum
in Udaipur, India.

See Maps of Museums and Art Sites, pages 144–147.

India

Growing and Changing

Something About Me

There's something about me
That I'm knowing.
There's something about me
That isn't showing.
I'm growing!

Anonymous

Unit Vocabulary

pattern	visual texture
rhythm	found objects
texture	

Multimedia Art Glossary
Visit *The Learning Site*
www.harcourtschool.com

Make Inferences

What do you see in this artwork?
What can you tell about the people?

Marisol Escobar, *The Family*

Use clues and what you already
know to make guesses about art.

Make a chart. Use clues to tell what you think.

What I See and Hear	+ What I Know =	What I Think

On Your Own

Look at the artwork on pages 62–63. Make a chart. Use clues. Tell what you think.

Patterns of Color

What stays the same in these artworks? What changes?

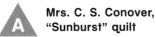 **Mrs. C. S. Conover, "Sunburst" quilt**

Lines, shapes, or colors that repeat make a **pattern**.

66

Tell about the patterns you see. How did the artists use colors and shapes?

B Seth, grade 2

"Kaleidoscope" Sponge Print

1. **Think about a pattern to make.**

2. **Use different colors. Make your pattern.**

Patterns in Clothing

What patterns do you see?
Lines, shapes, or colors that
repeat have a **rhythm**.

A Irene Lawson,
"Poke" Bonnet

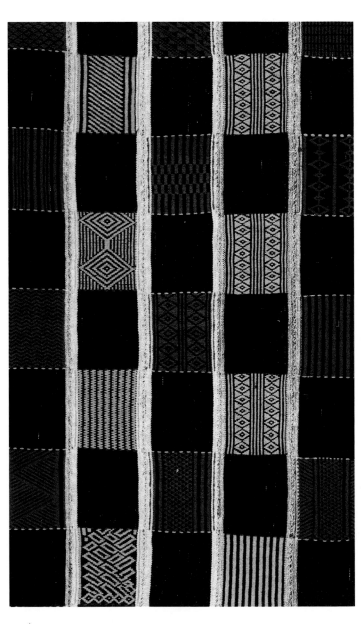

B Unknown artist (Dyula people,
Ivory Coast), Skirt detail

Paper Weaving

PLAN ....

Think about colors you want to put together.

CREATE ....

1. **Fold your paper in half. Cut eight slits.**

2. **Cut colored strips. Weave them. Draw designs.**

REFLECT ....

Use the word rhythm to tell about your weaving.

Tell two friends about the patterns you see on their clothes.

Judith Pinks,
Clothing Designer

Judith Pinks designs clothes for children. First she draws her ideas. Then she uses cloth with African patterns to make the clothes.

70

DID YOU KNOW?

Clothing designers often use animals or plants in their patterns. Can you find an animal in one of these designs?

Think About Art

How is designing clothes like painting? How is it different?

Textures We Can Touch

How would this bowl feel if you could touch it?

Unknown artist (New Guinea),
Bowl with handle

The way a thing feels is its **texture**.

| smooth | rough | bumpy | fluffy |

Textured Bowl

PLAN

Think of how your bowl will look and feel.

CREATE

1. **Roll a ball of clay. Push your thumbs in.**

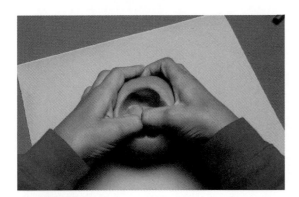

2. **Press out the sides. Add patterns and textures.**

REFLECT

How did you add texture to your bowl?

What different textures can you find in the classroom?

Textures We Can See

Tell what you see. How might these things feel?

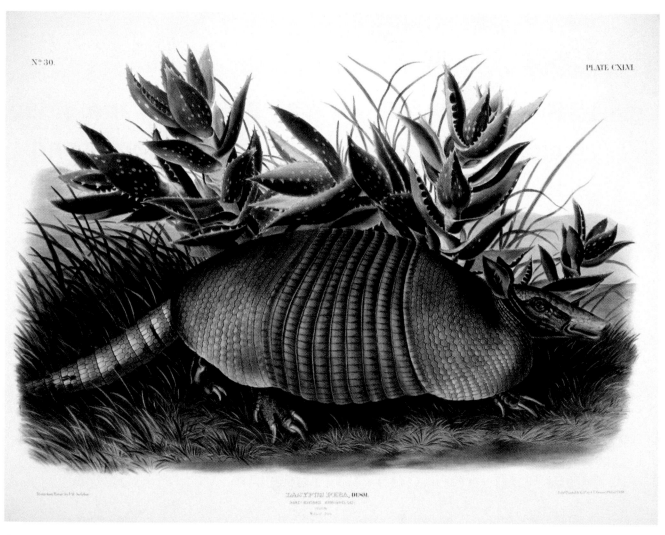

John James Audubon, *Armadillo*

Visual texture is how a thing looks as if it feels. What visual textures did the artist make?

Crayon Rubbing

PLAN ....

Find things with different textures.

CREATE ....

1. **Place a drawing on top of the things.**

2. **Rub the sides of crayons on top of the paper.**

REFLECT ....

Talk about the textures you see.

Look for visual textures in book illustrations.

Lucy Lewis's Pots

Lucy Lewis lived in the Acoma Pueblo in New Mexico. She made clay pots with Acoma patterns.

 A

Native North American vase with black-and-white pattern

Pot with deer, antelope, ram going around the sides **B**

DID YOU KNOW?

Each pueblo has its own style of pottery. Acoma Pueblo is known for its black-and-white patterns.

Think About Art

What can we learn about people by looking at the things they make?

Multimedia Biographies
Visit *The Learning Site*
www.harcourtschool.com

Textures We Can Build

What did the artists use to make these things?

Unknown artist,
Corn husk doll **A**

B Alexander Calder,
Dog

People make art with things they find, or **found objects**. Look at objects in a new way. What could you make?

78

Assemblage Toy

PLAN

Choose found objects you like.
Think of a toy to make.

CREATE

Glue the found
objects together
to make a toy.

REFLECT

How did you look at objects in a new way?

Unit 3 Review and Reflect

Tell which picture goes best with each word.

a.

b.

1. found objects

2. visual texture

3. pattern

c.

· ·

4. Tell about the rhythm in this picture.

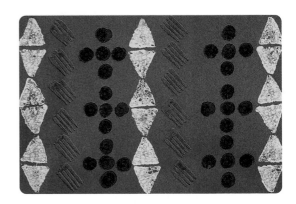

· ·

5. Use the word <u>texture</u> to tell about the picture.

Make Inferences

Look at the dog on page 78. Make a chart. Write what you think about the dog. Tell why.

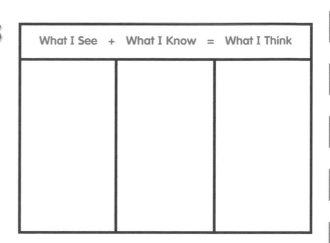

What I See	+	What I Know	=	What I Think

Write About Art

Write sentences about the animal and plants in this artwork. Tell what you think and why.

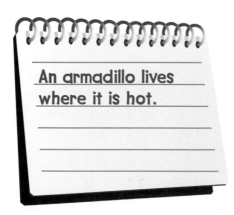

An armadillo lives where it is hot.

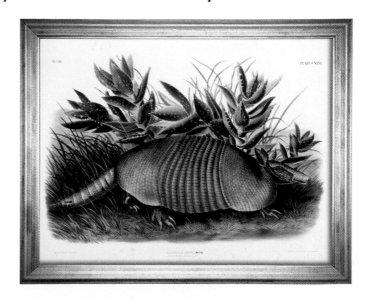

John James Audubon, *Armadillo*

▲ Ásmundur Sveinsson, Untitled sculpture

LOCATE IT

This sculpture is in the Ásmundur Sveinsson
Sculpture Museum in Reykjavík, Iceland.

See Maps of Museums and Art Sites, pages 144–147.

Imagine That!

Fun at the Playground

Swinging,

Swinging, way up high,

Stretching,

Stretching to touch the sky.

Around we go on the

merry-go-round,

Having fun at our playground.

from *Ring a Ring o' Roses*

Unit Vocabulary

forms	mobile
sculpture	landscape
architecture	horizon line
space	

ABOUT THE ARTIST

See Gallery of Artists, pages 184–191.

GO ONLINE

Multimedia Art Glossary
Visit *The Learning Site*
www.harcourtschool.com

Sequence

What is happening in these pictures? How can you tell?

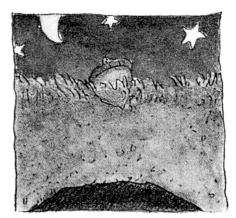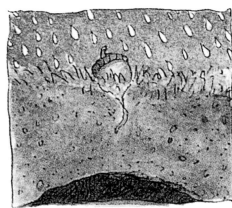

David McPhail, illustrations from *Mole Music* LITERATURE LINK

The order in which things happen is called **sequence**. A sequence tells what is first, next, and last.

Make a chart. Tell about the pictures on page 84. Use the words <u>first</u>, <u>next</u>, and <u>last</u>.

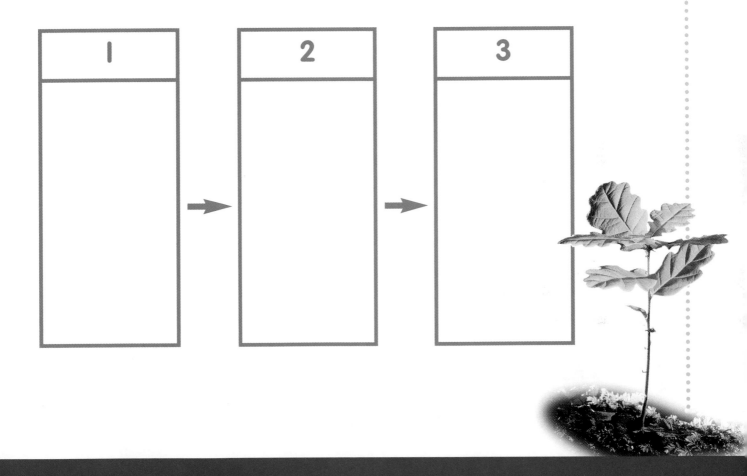

1	2	3

On Your Own

Imagine playing with the children on page 82. Make up a story. Tell what you would do first, next, and last.

Form and Shape

What shapes do you see? Shapes that take up space are called **forms**. Find forms in the art.

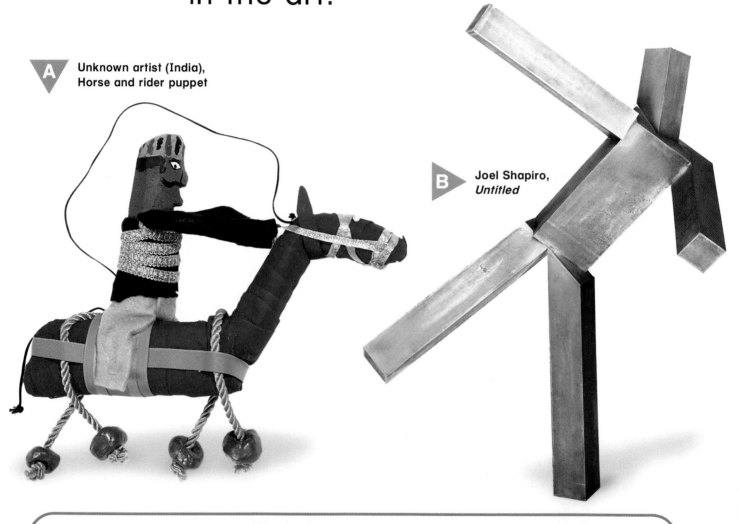

A Unknown artist (India),
Horse and rider puppet

B Joel Shapiro,
Untitled

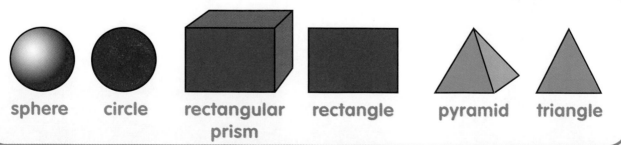

sphere   circle   rectangular prism   rectangle   pyramid   triangle

Story Puppet

PLAN

Think of a story character to make.

CREATE

1. Stuff a sock with paper. Make a head and arms.

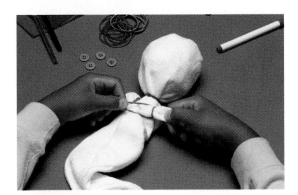

2. Add a face. Glue on hair. Add more details.

REFLECT

What story can you tell with your puppet?

What forms do you see around you?

Form in Sculpture

How are these artworks alike?

A ▼ Erykah, grade 1,
Mouse sculpture

B ▶ Unknown artist (Japan),
Caparisoned Haniwa Horse

A **sculpture** has form. It can be
seen from all sides. How might these
sculptures look from another side?

Clay Animal

PLAN

Choose an animal. Think about how it looks.

CREATE

1. Make the animal's body, head, and legs.

2. Add details to make your animal look real.

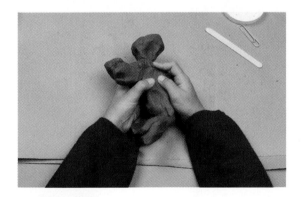 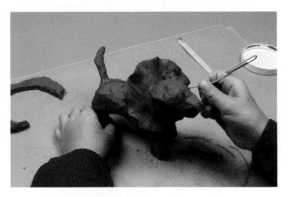

REFLECT

How is making a sculpture different from painting a picture?

Horses and Riders in Art

Artists make art about things that are important to them.

▼ **A** Jim Reno, *Dreams and Memories*

In many places, rodeo time is special. Horses, bulls, cowgirls, and cowboys are important parts of rodeos.

B Unknown artist (Mexico),
Mounted figure

Tell how all three artworks are alike.

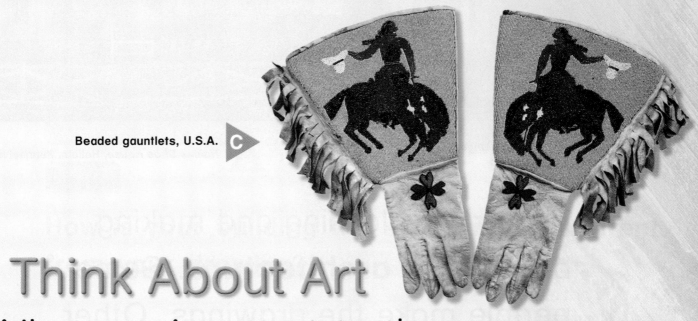

Beaded gauntlets, U.S.A. C

Think About Art

What was important to the artists who made these artworks? Why do you think so?

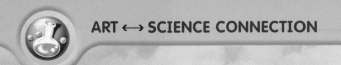
Alexander Calder's Mobiles

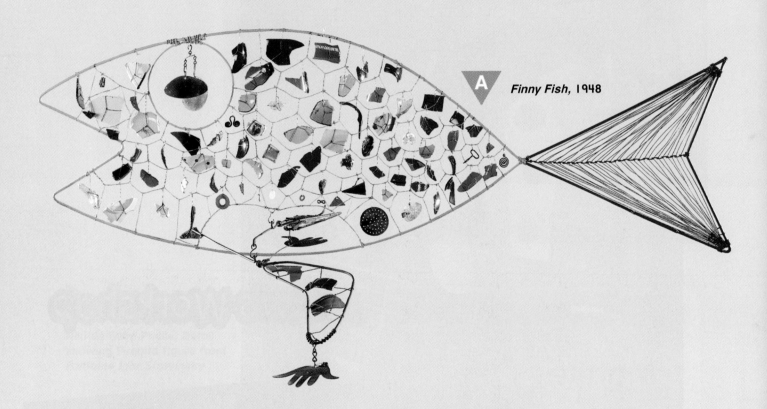

A **Finny Fish, 1948**

As a boy, Alexander Calder liked to make toys. He was the first artist to make mobiles. An artist friend named his sculptures <u>mobiles</u> because they moved.

Alexander Calder liked making
art that is fun to watch.

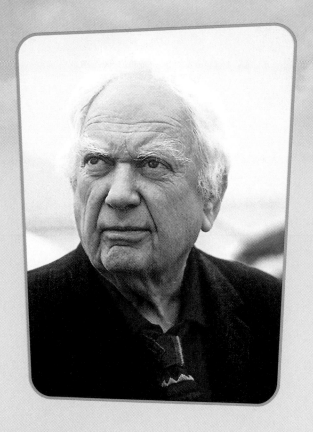

Think About Art

How is making a mobile
different from making
other sculptures?

B   *Ordinary, 1969*

GO ONLINE   **Multimedia Biographies**
Visit *The Learning Site*
www.harcourtschool.com

97

Space in Landscapes

What kinds of places do these artworks show?

A Robert S. Duncanson,
Landscape with Rainbow

A **landscape** shows a large outdoor place. It has a **horizon line** where the land and sky meet.

Find the horizon lines. How do the artworks show near and far?

 Emily, grade 1,
Landscape

Artist's Workshop

Landscape Painting

1. **Think of an outdoor place you like. Paint a horizon line.**

2. **Paint what you can see in that place.**

Unit 4 Review and Reflect

Vocabulary and Concepts

Tell which picture goes best with each word.

1. architecture

2. sculpture

3. mobile

a.

b.

c.

. . . .

4. Tell about the forms and spaces you see.

5. Tell about this picture. Use the words <u>horizon line</u> and <u>landscape</u>.

Sequence

Choose an artwork that you made in Unit 4. Tell how you made it. Make a flowchart. Show what you did first, next, and last.

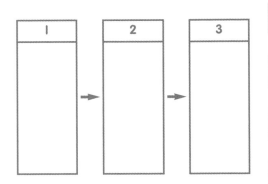

Write About Art

What would you do if you went to the place in this painting? Write what you would do first, next, and last.

First, I would run in the grass.

Robert S. Duncanson, *Landscape with Rainbow*

101

▲ Pierre-Auguste Renoir, *The Seine at Asnières*

LOCATE IT

This painting is in the National Gallery in London, England.

See Maps of Museums and Art Sites, pages 144–147.

England

Special Communities

Row, Row, Row Your Boat

Row, row, row your boat

Gently down the stream;

Merrily, merrily, merrily,

merrily,

Life is but a dream.

English Traditional Song

Unit Vocabulary

balance	abstract
symmetry	subject
emphasis	seascape

Multimedia Art Glossary
Visit *The Learning Site*
www.harcourtschool.com

ABOUT THE ARTIST

See Gallery of Artists, pages 184–191.

Draw Conclusions

What do you think these children are doing? What tells you?

Elizabeth Catlett,
Playmates

You can use clues in the artwork and what you know to help you decide.

Make a chart. Tell about clues in the art and what you hear. Tell what they help you decide.

Clues in Art and Reading	What I Decide

On Your Own

Look at the painting on pages 102–103. Make a chart. Write what you see and what you decide.

Balance in Nature

How are the two butterflies alike? How are they different?

Andy Warhol, *Butterfly*

Plants and animals show **balance** if they look the same on two sides. Find where each butterfly shows balance.

Butterfly Monoprint

PLAN ....

Think of shapes and colors for wings.

CREATE ....

1. **Fold your paper in half. Paint on one side only.**

2. **Fold the paper again. Press down. Open it.**

REFLECT ....

How does your print show balance?

Where else can you see things that have balance?

Balance in Art

Where do you see balance in these artworks?

 A Minnie Evans, *Design Made at Airlie Gardens*

Erykah, age 6 **B**

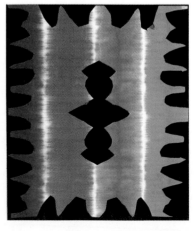

Art has **symmetry** when the shapes are the same on both sides.

Picture with Paper Cutouts

PLAN

Think about how to make a picture that shows symmetry.

CREATE

1. Cut out matching shapes. Glue one on each side.

2. Draw details. Make your work match on both sides.

REFLECT

How did you make both sides of your artwork the same?

Do you see something in your classroom that has symmetry?

Asian Kites

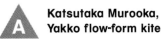 Katsutaka Murooka, Yakko flow-form kite

Kites were invented in China long, long ago. People in China, Korea, and Japan fly kites on special days. They also tell stories about kites.

110

B Chinese silk kite

Think About Art

Which kites show symmetry?

C Katsutaka Murooka, Thread kite and air bowl

Emphasis Using Color

What do you see first when you look at these paintings? The **emphasis** of an artwork is what you see first.

Joan Miró, *The Gold of the Azure*

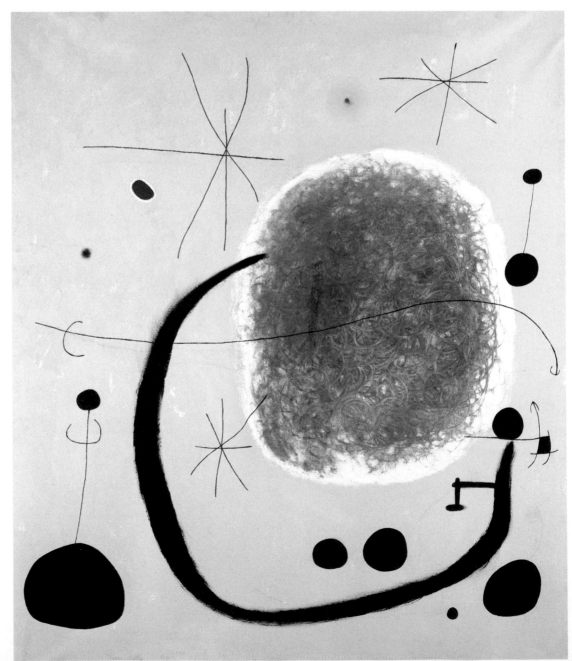

Both of these paintings are abstract. In **abstract** art, things may not look real.

 Alma Woodsey Thomas,
Atmospheric Effects II

Artist's Workshop

Music-Inspired Abstract Painting

Listen. Paint how the music makes you feel.

Emphasis Using Size

What is the biggest thing in this painting? Artists can use size to show emphasis. The **subject** of an artwork is what it is about.

Marc Chagall, *Green Violinist*

Self-Portrait with Stencil-Print Background

PLAN

Think of things you do in your neighborhood.

CREATE

1. Cut out stencils. Use them to make a neighborhood around the paper.

2. Paint yourself in the middle. Show something you like to do.

REFLECT

What does your painting tell about its subject?

CARMEN LOMAS GARZA'S
FAMILY

Carmen Lomas Garza grew up in Texas, near the border with Mexico. She paints pictures of her family. Her paintings are like stories about things she remembers.

A *Cumpleaños de Lala y Tudi*
(Lala's and Tudi's Birthday Party),
from *Family Pictures* LITERATURE LINK

 Autorretrato (Self-Portrait)

 **Sandía (Watermelon)**

THINK ABOUT ART

What can you learn about Carmen Lomas Garza's family by looking at her paintings?

GO ONLINE

Multimedia Biographies
Visit *The Learning Site*
www.harcourtschool.com

Emphasis in Seascapes

What places do these artworks show?

 A Edward Hopper,
Yawl Riding a Swell

 B Nicole, grade 2,
A Seascape

A **seascape** shows the sea. What else do you see in these seascapes?

118

Seascape Painting

PLAN ....

Think about things to show in your seascape.

CREATE ....

1. **Paint a horizon line. Paint water and the sky.**

2. **Add to your seascape. Make the water look as if it moves.**

REFLECT ....

Talk about the emphasis in your seascape and your classmates' seascapes.

What would you like to do at the sea?

119

Unit 5 Review and Reflect

Tell which picture goes best with each word.

1. seascape

2. symmetry

3. emphasis

a.

b.

c.

4. What is the subject of this picture?

5. Tell about the balance in this picture.

6. What makes this picture abstract?

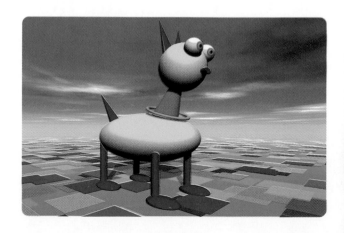

Draw Conclusions

Look at the larger painting on page 118. Use what you see and what you know to tell about it. Make a chart.

Clues in Art and Reading	What I Decide

Write About Art

Write about the painting below. Use what you see and what you know to write about the painting.

Two ladies are out rowing on a summer day.

Pierre-Auguste Renoir, *The Seine at Asnières*

▲ Lois Mailou Jones, *Pont Louis-Philippe, Paris*

LOCATE IT

This painting is in the Corcoran Gallery of Art in Washington, D.C.

See Maps of Museums and Art Sites, pages 144–147.

Washington, D.C.

Near and Far

A Friendship Bridge

I have a friend I've never seen;
    She lives in far Japan.
We write each other letters
    As often as we can.
It seems to me that letters
    Build a bridge across the sea
O'er which I go to visit her,
    And she comes to visit me!

Alice Crowell Hoffman

ABOUT THE ARTIST

See Gallery of Artists,
pages 184–191.

Unit Vocabulary

variety	montage
jewelry	origami
photograph	unity

Multimedia Art Glossary
Visit *The Learning Site*
www.harcourtschool.com

Variety in Our World

How are these artworks alike?
How are they different?

A Unknown artist (Yoruba people, Nigeria),
Headdress with face

B Unknown artist (Korea),
Box with ornaments

Artists give art **variety** by putting different lines, shapes, colors, or patterns together. Where do you see variety?

Parade Hat

PLAN

Think about a special hat.

CREATE

1. Bend your hat into a shape you like.

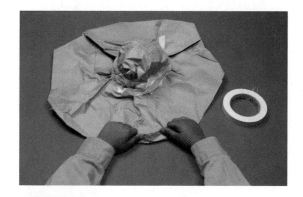

2. Decorate the hat with many things.

REFLECT

Compare hats. How do they show variety?

Where do you see variety around you?

127

Variety We Can Wear

Where do you see variety in these objects?

A Unknown artist (Flemish),
Butterfly jewel

B Johanna, age 6,
Necklace

C Unknown artist (Phoenician),
Necklace of glass beads

Necklaces, bracelets, and rings are kinds of **jewelry**. People around the world make and wear jewelry.

128

Paper-Bead Necklace

PLAN

Think about jewelry you want to make.

CREATE

1. **Draw patterns on paper strips. Roll them into beads. Glue.**

2. **String your beads together. Make a pattern.**

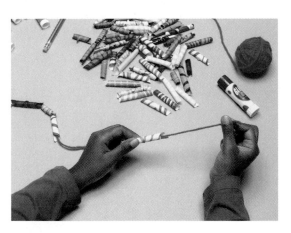

REFLECT

Tell a partner how you used pattern and variety.

Masks Around the World

People have always made and used masks. A mask can look like an animal, a person, or something else.

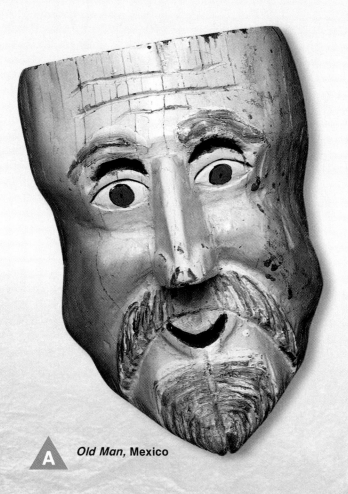

A *Old Man*, Mexico

B Helmet mask, Cameroon

130

Masks can be made of almost anything. Mask **B** is made of wood, metal, glass beads, fiber, and shells.

C Cat mask, Italy

D A mask representing the moon, Heiltsuk people, British Columbia, Canada

DID YOU KNOW?

People wear masks like mask **C** at parties. Mask **B** was made for a king to wear.

Think About Art

What story could you act out with one of these masks?

What the Camera Sees

What are these pictures about?
A **photograph** is made with a
camera. By pressing a button,
a person takes a picture.

Margaret Bourke-White,
The Statue of Liberty,
New York Harbor, 1952

Artists can put photographs together
to make a **montage**.

**Rich Frishman,
Untitled**

Artist's Workshop

Photo Montage

1. **Cut out pictures
   from magazines.**

2. **Put the pictures
   together. Glue.**

Paper Folding

What animals do you see here?

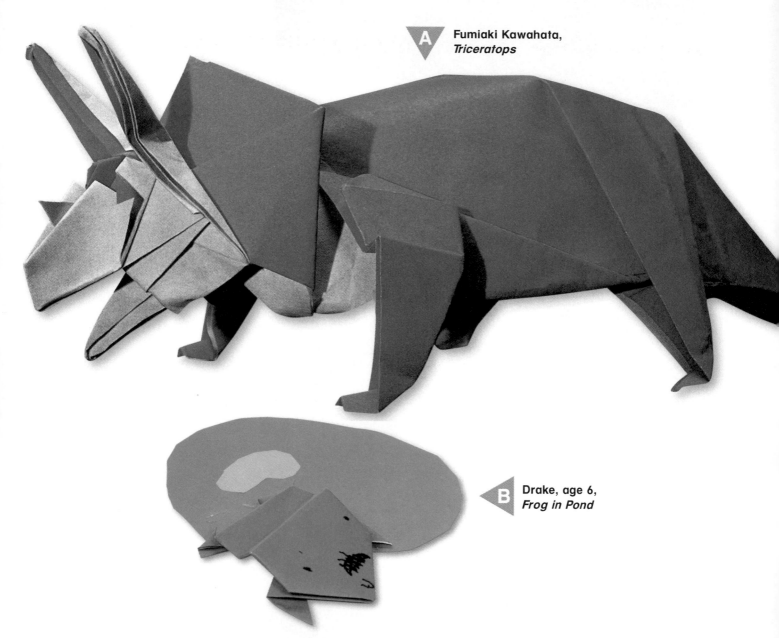

A ▽ Fumiaki Kawahata,
Triceratops

B ▷ Drake, age 6,
Frog in Pond

These animals are made of folded
paper. The art of folding paper is called
origami. It was first done in Asia.

134

Origami Animal

PLAN

Choose an animal you want to make.

CREATE

1. **Fold paper to make an animal.**

2. **Make a place for the animal to live.**

REFLECT

Was making your animal easy or hard to do? Why?

What are some other ways you use paper?

Faith Ringgold's Story Quilts

Faith Ringgold makes quilts that tell about her life. She paints the pieces and sews them together.

Tar Beach 2

After a quilt is put together, she writes the words.

 Sonny's Quilt

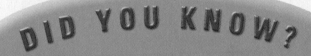

At first, Faith Ringgold was a painter. Then she started to work with fabric. She began to make quilts that were sewn and painted.

Think About Art

What do Faith Ringgold's quilts tell about people who are important to her?

Multimedia Biographies
Visit *The Learning Site*
www.harcourtschool.com

Celebration Art

How do these artworks make you think of celebrations?

 **Piñata, Mexico**

B Margit Kovács,
A Big Family

An artwork has **unity** when the parts seem to go together. Talk about the unity you see in the artworks.

Piñata

PLAN

Think of what to put in a piñata.

CREATE

1. **Stuff a bag with paper and treats. Tie it.**

2. **Cut designs in paper strips. Glue them to your piñata.**

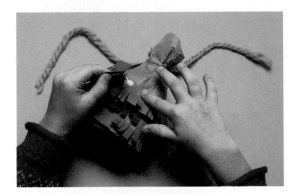

REFLECT

Why did you use the colors you did?

Look at book illustrations for pictures that have unity.

Unit 6 Review and Reflect

Tell which picture goes best with each word.

1. origami

2. jewelry

3. montage

4. photograph

a.

b.

c.

d.

• •

5. Use the words <u>variety</u> and <u>unity</u> to tell about this picture.

Main Idea

Look at the montage on page 133. Make a web. Tell details and the main idea.

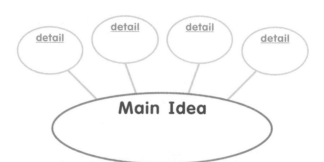

Write About Art

What is a main idea for this sculpture? Write a story about it.

Margit Kovács, *A Big Family*

141

Student Handbook

CONTENTS

10 Museums and Art Sites
United States

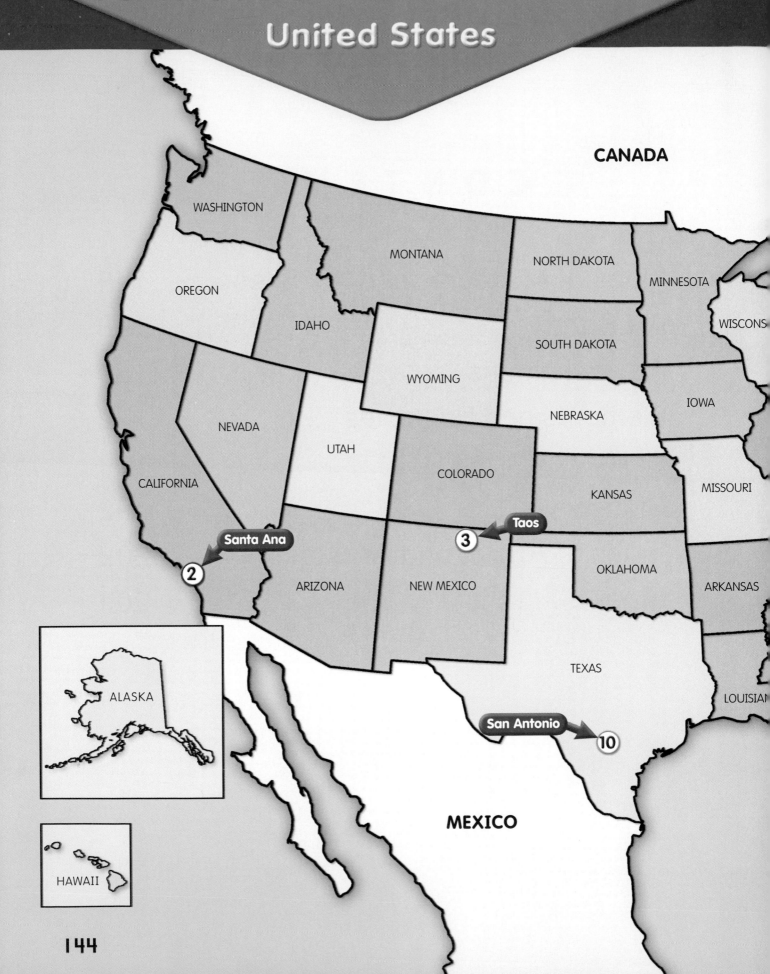

CANADA

WASHINGTON

MONTANA

NORTH DAKOTA

MINNESOTA

OREGON

IDAHO

WISCONS

WYOMING

SOUTH DAKOTA

NEVADA

UTAH

COLORADO

NEBRASKA

IOWA

CALIFORNIA

Santa Ana

2

KANSAS

MISSOURI

Taos

3

ARIZONA

NEW MEXICO

OKLAHOMA

ARKANSAS

ALASKA

TEXAS

LOUISIAN

San Antonio

10

MEXICO

HAWAII

Use the Electronic Art Gallery CD-ROM, Primary, to locate artworks from other museums and art sites.

MAINE

VERMONT

NEW HAMPSHIRE
MASSACHUSETTS

NEW YORK

New York City

RHODE ISLAND

CONNECTICUT

MICHIGAN

Cleveland

7

PENNSYLVANIA

INDIANA

OHIO

NEW JERSEY

4 9

DELAWARE
MARYLAND

ILLINOIS

Henderson

WEST
VIRGINIA

VIRGINIA

Washington, D.C.

6

KENTUCKY

TENNESSEE

NORTH CAROLINA

8

SOUTH
CAROLINA

Wilmington

GEORGIA

ALABAMA

Columbus

1

MISSISSIPPI

FLORIDA

N
W   E
S

LOCATE IT

See art for each of these sites on the pages shown.

(1) **Birthplace of Alma Woodsey Thomas,** page 113

(2) **Bowers Museum of Cultural Art,** page 77 (top)

(3) **City where Ernest Martin Hennings painted,** page 48

(4) **Corcoran Gallery of Art,** pages 122–123

(5) **One home of Edward Hopper,** page 118

(6) **John James Audubon State Park,** page 74

(7) **One of Margaret Bourke-White's studios, Terminal Tower,** page 132

(8) **Airlie Gardens, where Minnie Evans worked,** page 108

(9) **National Museum of Women in the Arts,** pages 22–23, 104

(10) **The Marion Koogler McNay Art Museum,** page 91 (top)

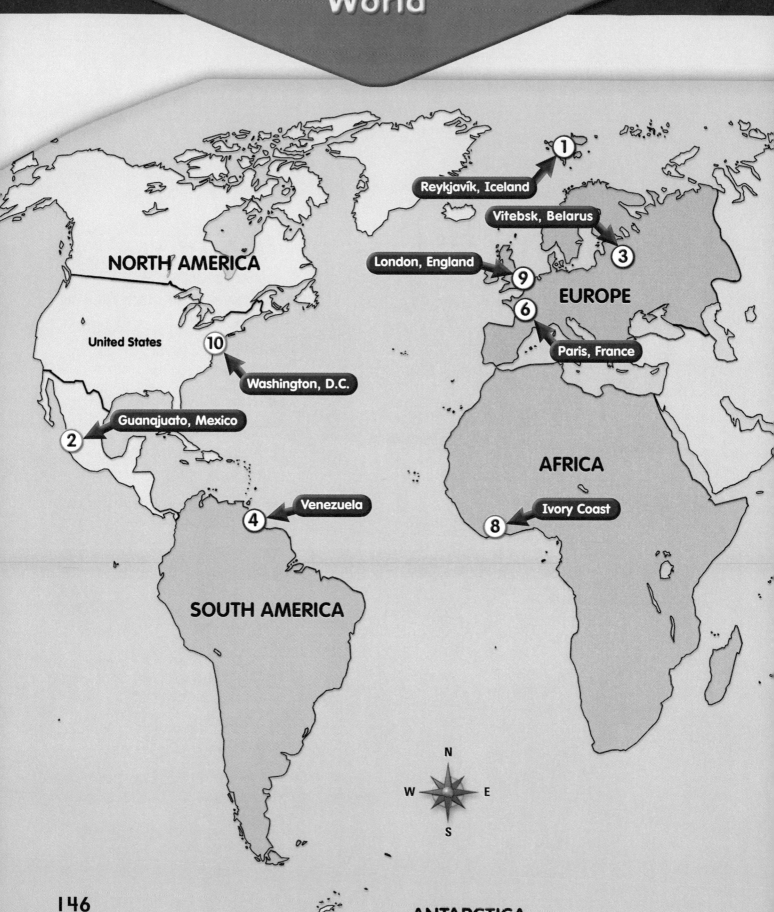

NORTH AMERICA

United States

Reykjavík, Iceland

Vitebsk, Belarus

London, England

9

3

6

EUROPE

Paris, France

10

Washington, D.C.

Guanajuato, Mexico

2

AFRICA

Venezuela

4

Ivory Coast

8

SOUTH AMERICA

N
W   E
S

ANTARCTICA

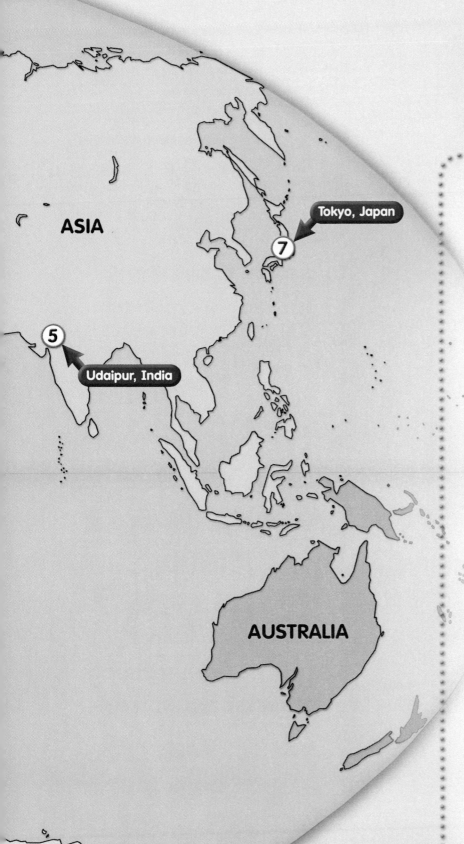

ASIA

Tokyo, Japan

⑦

⑤

Udaipur, India

AUSTRALIA

LOCATE IT

See art for each of these sites on the pages shown.

① **Ásmundur Sveinsson Sculpture Museum,** pages 82–83

② **Birthplace of Diego Rivera,** pages 50–51

③ **Birthplace of Marc Chagall,** pages 46, 114

④ **Birthplace of Marisol's parents, a place she often visited as a child,** page 64

⑤ **City Palace in Udaipur,** pages 62–63

⑥ **City where Renoir began as an artist,** pages 52, 102–103

⑦ **Home of Katsutaka Murooka, master kite builder,** pages 110–111

⑧ **Home of the Dyula artists,** page 68

⑨ **National Gallery in London,** pages 102–103

⑩ **Smithsonian American Art Museum,** pages 38, 42–43, 49, 98, 108, 113

Art Safety

Use only materials your teacher says are safe.

Use tools carefully. Keep them away from your face.

Wear a smock when you use messy materials.

Never run with scissors or other sharp objects.

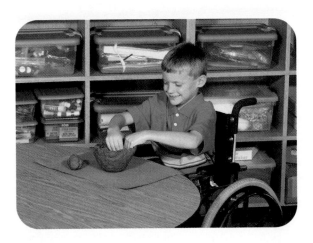

Keep art materials out of your mouth.

Clean up spills right away.

Keep the area around you neat.

Wash your hands after making art.

DRAWING
Pencil

Press lightly to make light lines.

Press harder to make dark lines.

Tilt the tip to make thick lines.

Make dots with the tip.

DRAWING
Markers

You can make dots
and circles.

Make thin lines with
the tip.

Use the side to make
thick lines.

Put the cap on when
you are done.

DRAWING
Crayons

Make thin lines and dots with the tip.

Tilt the tip to make thick lines.

Make big dots with the bottom.

Color big spaces with the side.

DRAWING
Oil Pastels

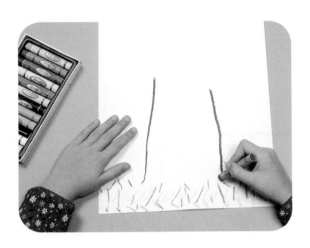

Make light and dark lines.

Color big spaces with the side.

Blend colors with a paper towel.

Add colors on top of other colors.

PAINTING
Mixing Colors

1. Dip the brush in a color. Put the paint on a plate or tray.

2. Rinse the brush. Blot. Dip it into another color.

3. Mix the colors. Use the new color.

4. Rinse and blot between colors.

PAINTING
Tempera

Use a wide brush
for thick lines and
big spaces.

Use a thin brush
for details.

Try making short, fast
strokes.

Try holding your brush
different ways. See
what kinds of lines
you can make.

PAINTING
Watercolor

1. Drip water onto each color. Get paint on the brush.

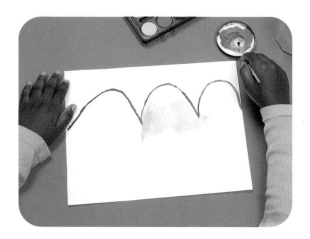

2. Mix colors on a tray or plate.

Press hard to make thick lines. Press lightly to make thin lines.

Paint on wet paper. Make a wash.

PAINTING
Crayon Resist

1. Draw with crayons or oil pastels.

2. Color the picture. Press hard.

3. Paint over the drawing with watercolors.

4. The drawing shows through.

CLAY
Pinch Pot

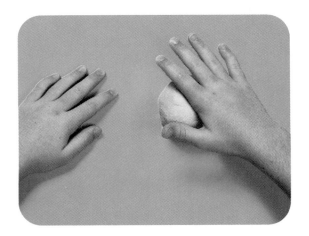

1. Roll clay into a ball.

2. Push down in the middle with your thumbs.

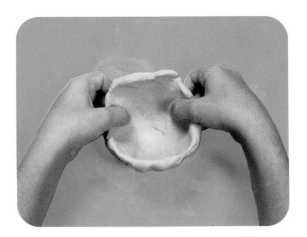

3. Pull up the sides. Try to make them even.

4. Smooth out the sides.

158

CLAY
Sculpture

1. Roll clay into an oval.

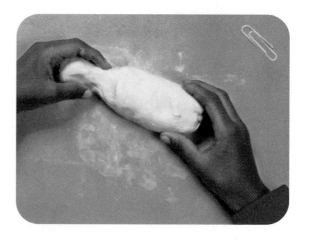

2. Pull out a part for the head.

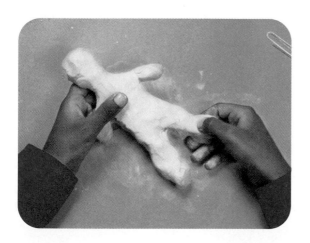

3. Pull out parts for the arms and legs. Make the legs thick.

4. Smooth out the sculpture. Add details.

PRINTMAKING
Sponge Prints

1. Cut shapes from a sponge.

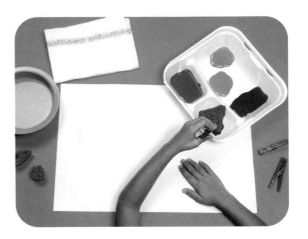

2. Wet the sponge. Dip it in paint.

3. Press onto paper.

4. Use a new sponge for each color.

PRINTMAKING
Stencils

1. Draw shapes on thick paper.

2. Cut them out from the inside.

Paint inside the stencil with a brush.

Paint inside the stencil with a sponge.

PRINTMAKING
Foam Tray Prints

1. Draw on a tray with a pencil. Press hard.

2. Roll on a little ink or paint.

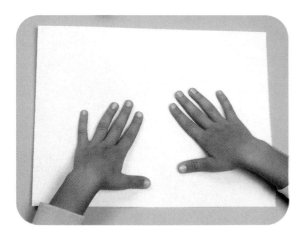

3. Press paper over the tray.

4. Carefully lift the paper.

PRINTMAKING
Monoprint

1. Paint on paper or plastic.

2. Lay paper over the painting.

3. Press the paper onto the painting.

4. Carefully lift off the paper.

WEAVING
Paper Loom

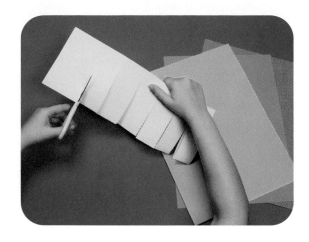

1. Fold paper in half. Cut wide slits.

2. Cut strips of paper.

3. Weave under and over.

4. Continue to weave over and under.

WEAVING
Paper Plate Loom

1. Cut slits in a paper plate.

2. Wrap yarn in the slits.

3. Start in the middle.

4. Weave around, going over and under.

COLLAGE
Mixed Media

1. Cut or tear paper.

2. Use cloth, ribbons, and found objects.

3. Place the things where you want them.

4. Glue.

MOSAIC
Paper

1. Cut or tear paper into pieces.

2. Place the pieces. Make a picture or pattern.

3. Leave small spaces between the pieces.

4. Glue.

PAPER FOLDING
How to Make a Square

1. Start with a rectangle.

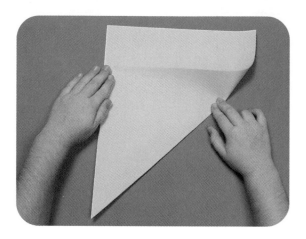

2. Fold the long side. Make the edges touch.

3. Draw a pencil line. Cut along the line.

4. Open.

PAPER FOLDING

3-D Paper Forms
Cones

1. Start with a circle.
Cut to the middle.

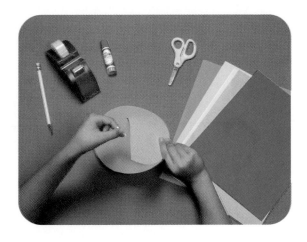

2. Fold one part
under the cut.
Tape or glue.

Paper Strip Forms

Fold paper back and
forth. Shape into forms.

Bend paper into
rounded forms.

PAPER FOLDING
Origami Dog

1. Fold the paper in half.

2. Fold down one ear.

3. Fold down the other ear.

4. Fold up the bottom corner.

PAPER FOLDING
Origami Rabbit

1. Fold paper in half.

2. Fold up the long side.

3. Fold up the two sides. Turn over.

4. Fold the top corner behind.

Line

thin ▼

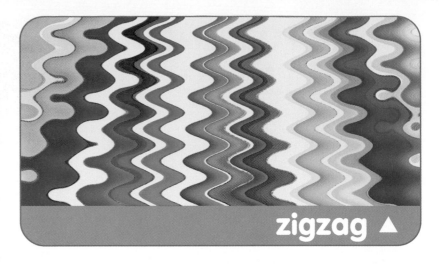

zigzag ▲

curved ▲

thick ▲

diagonal ▼

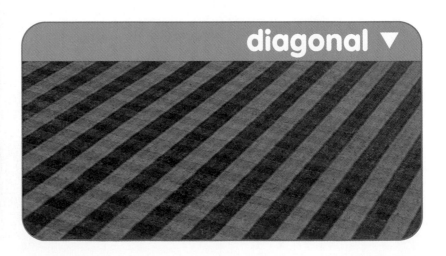

Shape

oval ▲

rectangle ▲

free form ▼

triangle ▼

YIELD

organic ▼

square ▲

173

Color and Value

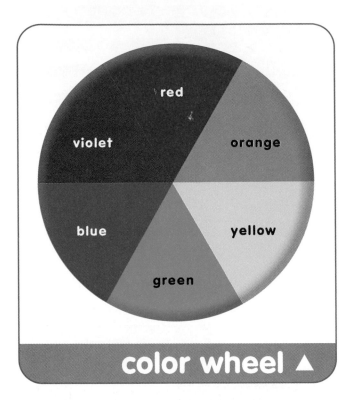

color wheel ▲

brown ▲

neutral colors ▲

value ▲

warm colors ▲

cool colors ▲

Texture

fluffy ▲

bumpy ▼

rough ▲

soft ▼

smooth ▲

scratchy ▼

Form

sphere ▼

cube ▼

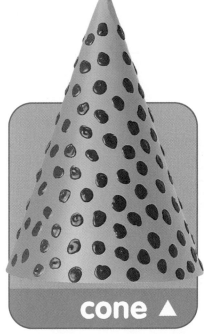

cone ▲

free form ▲

pyramid ▼

Space

positive space

negative space

horizon line

horizon line

background

foreground

Pattern

179

Rhythm and Movement

Emphasis

Variety and Unity

variety ▲

variety ▼

unity ▲

Gallery of Artists

John James Audubon

(1785–1851) page 74

Eric Carle

(1929–) pages 56, 57

Margaret Bourke-White

(1904–1971) page 132

Elizabeth Catlett

(1915–) page 104

Alexander Calder

(1898–1976) pages 26, 78, 95, 96

Paul Cézanne

(1839–1906) page 35

Marc Chagall

(1887–1985) pages 46, 114

Marisol Escobar

(1930–) page 64

Mrs. C. S. Conover

(b. 1788) page 66

Minnie Evans

(1892–1987) page 108

Robert S. Duncanson

(1821–1872) page 98

Rich Frishman

(1951–) page 133

Gallery of Artists

Carmen Lomas Garza
(1948–) pages 24, 116, 117

Edward Hopper
(1882–1967) page 118

Ernest Martin Hennings
(1886–1956) page 48

William H. Johnson
(1901–1970) page 38

Nancy Hom
(1949–) page 44

Lois Mailou Jones
(1905–1998) page 122

Fumiaki Kawahata

(1957–) page 134

Margit Kovács

(1902–1977) page 138

Rockwell Kent

(1882–1971) page 49

Adélaïde Labille-Guiard

(1749–1803) page 54

Paul Klee

(1879–1940) page 32

Irene Lawson

page 68

Gallery of Artists

Lucy Lewis

(c. 1897–1992) pages 76, 77

Henri Matisse

(1869–1954) page 26

David McPhail

(1940–) page 84

Joan Miró

(1893–1983) page 112

Gabriele Münter

(1877–1962) page 22

Katsutaka Murooka

(1941–) pages 110, 111

Georgia O'Keeffe

(1887–1986) page 29

Pablo Picasso

(1881–1973) page 38

Judith Pinks

(1952–) pages 70, 71

Maurice Prendergast

(1858–1924) page 42

Jim Reno

(1929–) page 90

Pierre-Auguste Renoir

(1841–1919) pages 52, 102

Gallery of Artists

Faith Ringgold

(1930–) pages 136, 137

Diego Rivera

(1886–1957) pages 50, 51

Niki de Saint Phalle

(1930–2002) page 94

Joel Shapiro

(1941–) page 86

Ásmundur Sveinsson

(1893–1982) page 82

Alma Woodsey Thomas

(1891–1978) page 113

Mai Thu

(1906–1980) page 124

Vincent van Gogh

(1853–1890) pages 28, 30, 31

Andy Warhol

(1928–1987) page 106

Anna Belle Lee Washington

(1924–2000) page 54

Glossary

abstract

Art with parts that may not look real. (page 113)

architecture

The art of planning and making buildings. (page 92)

art

Things that are made to be looked at or experienced. Examples are paintings, drawings, and sculptures. (page 26)

artist

A person who makes art. (page 26)

artwork

A piece of art. (page 32)

balance

The way parts of an artwork work together so that the parts seem equal. (page 106)

beads

Small pieces of material with holes for string. (page 129)

camera

A machine that uses light to take pictures. (page 132)

colors

Red, orange, yellow, green, blue, violet. (page 46)

color wheel

A chart that shows colors in the order of the rainbow. (page 47)

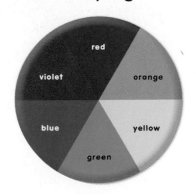

193

cool colors

Colors that give a cool feeling, such as green, blue, and violet. (page 49)

emphasis

The part of an artwork that you see first. (page 112)

form

A shape that takes up space and can be seen from all sides. (page 86)

found objects

Objects that can be used in a new way to make art. (page 78)

free-form shapes

Shapes that are not math shapes, such as the shapes of animals and many plants. (page 34)

horizon line

The place in a picture where land or water meets the sky. (page 98)

jewelry

Art that people wear, such as necklaces and rings. (page 128)

landscape

A picture that shows an outdoor place. (page 98)

lines

Marks that have length and direction. (page 26)

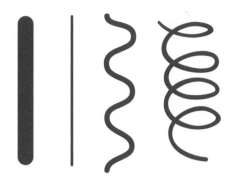

mask

A covering for the face. (page 130)

mobile

A kind of sculpture that can move. (page 95)

montage

A picture made by putting together many pictures or patterns. (page 133)

mural

A large painting done on a wall. (page 50)

origami

The art of folding paper into shapes. (page 134)

painter

An artist who paints. (page 30)

painting

An artwork made with paint. (page 24)

pattern

Lines, shapes, or colors that repeat. (page 66)

photograph

A picture made using a camera. (page 132)

piñata

A decorated container that is filled with treats. At parties, children try to break the piñata open with a stick. (page 138)

portrait

A picture of one or more people. (page 38)

pottery

Objects such as bowls made from clay and hardened. (page 77)

rhythm

Repeating lines, shapes, or colors that give a sense of movement. (page 68)

sculpture

An artwork that has form and can be seen from all sides. (page 88)

seascape

A picture that shows the
sea. (page 118)

self-portrait

An artist's picture of
himself or herself.
(page 38)

shade

A darker color made by
adding black to a color.
(page 54)

shapes

Flat, closed spaces.
(page 32)

space

Empty parts within or
around an artwork.
(page 94)

stained glass

Pieces of colored glass
that make pictures or
patterns. (page 58)

still life

An artwork showing a group of things that are not moving. (page 35)

subject

What an artwork is about. (page 114)

symmetry

The balance in an artwork when both sides are the same. (page 108)

texture

The way something feels. (page 72)

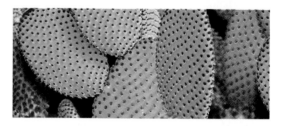

tint

A lighter color made by adding white to a color. (page 52)

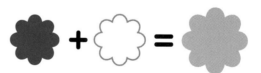

unity

An artwork has unity when all the parts seem to go together. (page 138)

value

The lightness or darkness of a color. (page 52)

variety

Many colors, shapes, or kinds of lines together in an artwork. (page 126)

visual texture

The way something looks as if it would feel. (page 74)

warm colors

Colors that give a warm feeling, such as red, orange, and yellow. (page 48)

zigzag

A line with sharp turns. (page 28)

Index of Artists and Artworks

Index

Index

Acknowledgments

For permission to reprint copyrighted material, grateful acknowledgment is made to the following sources:

Flint Public Library, 1026 East Kearsley, Flint, MI 48502-1994: From "Fun at the Playground" in *Ring a Ring o' Roses: Finger Plays for Pre-School Children,* 11th Edition. Text copyright 1996 by Flint Public Library.

Harcourt, Inc.: Untitled poem (Titled: "From My Window") from *Poems of Childhood* by Joan Walsh Anglund. Text copyright © 1996 by Joan Walsh Anglund. From *Feathers for Lunch* by Lois Ehlert. Copyright © 1990 by Lois Ehlert.

Philomel Books, A division of Penguin Young Readers Group, A Member of Penguin Group (USA) Inc., 345 Hudson St., New York, NY 10014: Cover illustration from *Today Is Monday* by Eric Carle. Illustration copyright © 1993 by Eric Carle.

Random House Children's Books, a division of Random House, Inc., New York, NY: "Something About Me" by anonymous from *Read-Aloud Rhymes for the Very Young,* selected by Jack Prelutsky.

Scholastic Inc.: "A Friendship Bridge" by Alice Crowell Hoffman from *Poetry Place Anthology.* Text copyright © 1983 by Edgell Communications, Inc.

Photo Credits

Page Placement Key: (t)-top (c)-center (b)-bottom (l)-left (r)-right

All photos property of Harcourt except for the following:

Frontmatter

5 (tl) Erich Lessing/Art Resource, NY; (tc) Arthur Thevenart/Corbis; 6 (tl) Dinodia; (tr) The Newark Museum/Art Resource, NY; 7 (tl) © 2006 Estate of Alexander Calder/Artists Rights Society (ARS), New York/Art Resource, NY; 8 (tr) The Art Archive/Palazzo Pitti Florence/Dagli Orti; 9 (tl) © 2006 Artist Rights Society (ARS), New York/HUNGART, Budapest; 11 (tl) The Newark Museum/Art Resource, NY; 12 Lois Ehlert; 14 (t) Dennis Marsico/Corbis; (b) Richard T. Nowitz Photography; 15 (t) Kelly-Mooney Photography/Corbis; (b) David Butow/Corbis SABA; 16 (t) © 2006 Artist Rights Society (ARS), New York/VG Bild-Kunst, Bonn/Giraudon/Art Resource; 19 (tr) Alamy Images; (tl) Getty Images; 20 William Manning/Corbis; (tr) John Warden/SuperStock; 21 (br) Alamy Images.

Unit 1

22 © 2006 Artists Rights Society (ARS), New York/VG Bild-Kunst, Bonn/Gabriele Munter (German, 1877-1962), Staffelsee in Autumn, 1923. Oil on Board 13 3/4 X 19 1/4 in. The National Museum of Women in The Arts. Gift of Wallace and Whilhelmina Holladay; 23 (b) © 2006 Artists Rights Society (ARS), New York/VG Bild-Kunst, Bonn/Princeton University Art Museum. Gift of Frank E. Taplin, Jr., Class of 1937, and Mrs. Taplin; 24 Copyright 1991 Carmen Lomas Garza/Photo by Judy Reed/Collection of Romeo; 26 (l) © 2006 Estate of Alexander Calder/Artists Rights Society (ARS), New York/Art Resource, NY; (r) © 2006 Succession H. Matisse, Paris/Artists Rights Society (ARS), New York/Bridgeman-Giraudon/Art Resource, NY; 28 (t) Warwick Kent/Photolibrary/PictureQuest; (b) The Museum of Modern Art/Licensed by Scala/Art Resource, NY; 29 (t) © 2006 The Georgia O'Keeffe Foundation/Artist Rights Society (ARS), New York/Collection of the McNay Art Museum, Gift of the Estate of Tom Slick; 30 Art Institute of Chicago/Helen Birch Bartlett Memorial Collection/SuperStock; 31 (t) Reunion des Musees Nationaux/Art Resource, NY; (b) Bridgeman Art Library; 32 (t) © 2006 Artists Rights Society (ARS), New York/VG Bild-Kunst, Bonn/Bridgeman-Giraudon/Art Resource, NY; 34 Hannah Sellers/St. Brigid of Kildare, Dublin, OH; 35 (t) Courtauld Institute Gallery, Somerset House, London/The Bridgeman Art; 37 (l) Index Stock Imagery, Inc.; 38 (l) © 2006 Estate of Pablo Picasso/Artists Rights Society (ARS), New York/Private Collection AKG, Berlin/SuperStock; 40 (left to right, 4) Alamy Images; (10) Gay Bumgarner/Index stock Photography; 41 The Museum of Modern Art/Licensed by Scala/Art Resource, NY.

Unit 2

42 Smithsonian American Art Museum, Washington, DC / Art Resource, NY; 43 (b) Williams College Museum of Art; 44 Children's Book Press; 46 © 2006 Artist Rights Society (ARS), New York/ADAGP, Paris/The Museum of Modern Art/Licensed by SCALA/Art Resource, NY; 48 Collection Fred Jones Jr. Museum of Art, The University of Oklahoma, Purchase, Richard h. and Adeline J. Fleischaker Collection, 1996; 49 (t) Smithsonian American Art Museum, Washington, DC/Art Resource, NY; 50 Art Resource, NY; 51 (t) Mexican Government; (b) Benjamin Blackwell/University of California, Berkeley, Stern Hall; bequest of Mrs. Sigmund Stern; 52 © The Barnes Foundation, Merion Station, Pennsylvania/Corbis; 54 (l) Anna Belle Lee Washington/Superstock; (r) The Bridgeman Art Library; 56 (t) From "Today is Monday." Illustration Copyright 1993 by Eric Carle; All Rights Reserved; 57 (b) From "Today is Monday." Illustration Copyright 1993 by Eric Carle; All Rights Reserved; (t) Motoko Inoue/Eric Carle Studio; 58 (l) Bibi Singh/P.S. 123K, Brooklyn, NY; (r) Arthur Thevenart/Corbis; 60 (tl) Arthur Thevenart/Corbis; 61 Anna Belle Lee Washington/Superstock.

Unit 3

62 Dinodia; 64 Digital Image (c) The Museum of Modern Art/Licensed by SCALA/Art/ Licensed by VAGA, New York, NY; 66 The Newark Museum/Art Resource, NY; 67 (t) Seth Carpenter/Viking Elementary, Pelican rapids, MN; 68 (l) Dean Beasom/National Gallery of Art; (r) The Newark Museum/Art Resource, NY; 70 Lisa Quinones/Black Star/Harcourt; 71 Judith Pinks; 72 (t) Schomburg Center, The New York Public Library/Art Resource, NY; 74 Academy of Natural Sciences of Philadelphia/Corbis; 76 Jerry Jacka Photography; 77 (t) Bowers Museum of Cultural Art/Corbis; (b) Lucy Lewis/Courtesy of King Galleries of Scottsdale; 78 © 2006 Estate of Alexander Calder/Artists Rights Society (ARS), New York/Art Resource, NY; 81 Academy of Natural Sciences of Philadelphia/Corbis.

Acknowledgments

Unit 4

82 Paul Almay/Corbis; 83 (b) Reykjavik Art Museum; 84 David McPhail/Henry Holt and Company; 85 S. Dalton/Photo Researchers; 86 (l) Designed by Meryl Doney/ Harcourt; (r) Christie's Images/Corbis; 88 (l) Erykah Wilson; (r) The Cleveland Museum of Art; 90 Dreams and Memories by Jim Reno; 91 (t) Rhonda Hole/National Cowgirl Museum; (b) San Antonio Museum of Art, Nelson A. Rockefeller Mexican Folk Art Collection; 92 (l) Angelo Cavalli/Superstock; (r) Ruth Miller; 94 © 2006 Artists Rights Society (ARS), New York/ADAGP, Paris/Stefano Bianchetti/Corbis; 95 (t) © 2006 Estate of Alexander Calder/Artists Rights Society (ARS), New York/Whitney Museum of American Art, New York; purchase, with funds from the Howard and Jean Lipman Foundation; 96 © 2006 Estate of Alexander Calder/Artists Rights Society (ARS), New York/Gift of Mr. and Mrs. Klaus G. Perls/National Gallery of Art, Washington; 97 (t) Jean Gaumy/Magnum Photos; (b) © 2006 Estate of Alexander Calder/Artists Rights Society (ARS), New York/Art Resource, NY; 98 Smithsonian American Art Museum, Washington, DC/Art Resource, NY; 99 (t) Emily Roebuck/McKinley Elementary, Davenport, IA; 101 Smithsonian American Art Museum, Washington, DC/Art Resource, NY.

Unit 5

102 National Gallery Collection; By kind permission of the Trustees of the National Gallery, London/Corbis; 103 (b) Francis G. Mayer/Corbis; 104 Elizabeth Catlett/Licensed by VAGA, New York, NY; 106 (r) © 2006 Andy Warhol Foundation for the Visual Arts/ARS, New York/Bass Museum of Art/Corbis; 108 (t) Smithsonian American Art Museum, Washington, DC/Art Resource, NY; (b) Erykah Wilson/Harcourt; 110 (l) (b) Katsutaka Murooka; 112 © 2006 Succession Miro/Artists Rights Society (ARS), New York/ADSGP, Paris/Archivo Iconografico, S.A./Corbis/Artists Rights Society (ARS), New York; 113 (t) Smithsonian American Art Museum, Washington, DC/Art Resource, NY; 114 © 2006 Artist Rights Society (ARS), New York/ADAGP, Paris/Solomon R. Guggenheim Museum, New York; 116 Copyright 1989 Carmen Lomas Garza/Wolfgang Dietze/Collection of Paula Maciel; 117 (t) Copyright 1980 Carmen Lomas Garza/Wolfgang Dietze/Collection of the artist; (b) Copyright 1986 Carmen Lomas Garza/Wolfgang Dietze/Collection of Dudley D. Brooks & Tomas Ybarra-frausto, New York, NY; 118 (t) Worcester Art Museum; (b) Nicole/Eugene Field Elementary, Maryville, MO; 121 National Gallery Collection; By kind permission of the Trustees of the National gallery, London/Corbis.

Unit 6

122 The Corcoran Gallery of Art/Corbis; 124 The Art Archive/Private Collection Paris/Dagli Orti; 126 (l) The Art Archive/Ethnic Jewelry Exhibition Milan/Dagli Orti; (r) The Newark Museum/Art Resource, NY; 128 (tl) The Art Archive/Palazzo Pitti Florence/Dagli Orti; (r) Scala/Art Resource, NY; (bl) Johanna Bender/Harcourt; 130 (r) San Antonio Museum of Art, Nelson A. Rockefeller Mexican Folk Art Collection; (l) The Metropolitan Museum of Art, The Michael C. Rockefeller Memorial; 131 (tr) Werner Forman/Art Resource, NY; (l) Ed Bohon/Corbis; 132 Margaret Bourke-White/Timepix; 133 (t) Getty Images; 134 (t) Folded by Alex Barber, Photo by Tracy Vessels, Model Designed by Fumiaki; (b) Drake William/Harcourt; 136 (b) Faith Ringgold; 137 (t) Grace Matthews 2000; (b) Faith Ringgold; 138 (l) Richard Cummins/Corbis; (r) © 2006 Artists Rights Society (ARS), New York/HUNGART, Budapest/Margit Kovacs; 140 (tr) Royalty-Free/Corbis; 141 Margit Kovacs;

Elements of Art

172 (tr) Getty Images; (br) Chase Swift/Corbis 176 (br) Royalty-Free/Corbis.

Gallery of Artists

Audubon: Bettmann/Corbis; Bourke-White: AP/Wide World Photos; Calder: Jean Gaumy/Magnum Photos; Carle: Motoko Inoue/Eric Carle Studio; Catlett: Charles Storer/June Kelly Gallery; Cezanne: Erich Lessing/Art Resource, NY; Chagall: Martine Franck/Magnum Photos; Duncanson: Notman Photographic Archives/McCord Museum of Canadian History; Escobar: Christopher Felver/Corbis; Evans: Courtesy of Louise Wells Cameron Art Museum/Jo Kallenborn; photograph by Jack Dermid; Frishman: Frish Photo; Garza: Dale Higgins/Harcourt; Hennings: Courtesy Museum of New Mexico, #20116/Museum of New Mexico; Hom: Bob Hsiang/BH Photography; Hopper: National Portrait Gallery, Smithsonian Institution/Art Resource, NY; Johnson: Smithsonian American Art Museum, Washington, DC/The Art Resource, NY; Kawahata: Fumiaki Kawahata; Kent: Bettmann/Corbis; Klee: Hulton Archives/Getty Images; Kovacs: Varosi Muveszeti Muzeum-Borsos Miklos Archivum, Gyor/Varosi Muveszeti; Lewis: Jerry Jacka Photography; Matisse: © 2006 Succession H. Matisse, Paris/Artists Rights Society (ARS), New York /AKG Images; McPhail: Jan L. Waldron/David McPhail; Miro: James A. Sugar/Corbis; Munter: © 2006 Artists Rights Society (ARS), New York/VG Bild-Kunst, Bonn/Princeton University Art Museum. Gift of Frank E. Taplin, Jr., Class of 1937, and Mrs. Taplin; O'Keeffe: National Portrait Gallery, Smithsonian Institution/Art Resource, NY; Picasso: © 2006 Estate of Pablo Picasso/Artists Rights Society (ARS), New York/Philadelphia Museum of Art/Corbis; Pinks: Lisa Quinones/Black Star/Harcourt; Prendergast: Williams College Museum of Art; Reno: Jim Reno; Renior: Francis G. Mayer/Corbis; Sveinsson: Reykjavik Art Museum; Saint Phalle: Christopher Felver/Corbis; Thomas: Smithsonian American Art Museum, Washington, DC/Art Resource, NY; Ringgold: Grace Matthews/FaithRinggold.com; Rivera: Bettmann/Corbis; Van Gogh: Reunion des Musees Nationaux/Art Resource, NY; Warhol: Corbis; Anna Belle Lee Washington: Anna Belle Lee Washington.

Glossary

192 (cr) Alamy Images; 194 (bl) Almay Images; 195 (cr) (br) Alamy Images; 197 (tr) Kactus Foto, Santiago, Chile/SuperStock; (bl) (cr) Almay Images; 198 (tl) Getty Images; (tr) Alan Schein Photography/Corbis; 199 (br) Alamy Images; 200 (cl) Tretyakov Gallery Moscow/AKG Berlin/SuperStock; (bl)Corbis; (br) Philip Harvey/Corbis.